# IT'S A FACT! Real-Life Reads

# Horrible ANIMAL Habits

by Ruth Owen

**Consultant:**

**Suzy Gazlay, MA**
Recipient, Presidential Award for Excellence in Science Teaching

*Ruby Tuesday Books*

Published in 2014 by Ruby Tuesday Books Ltd.

Editor: Mark J. Sachner
Designer: Emma Randall
Production: John Lingham

Photo Credits:
Alamy: 12–13, 20–21; Diomedia: 25; FLPA: 4 (bottom), 5 (bottom), 8–9,
16–17; Science Photo Library: 4 (top); Shutterstock: Cover, 5 (top), 6–7, 9
(center), 10–11, 14–15, 17 (top), 18–19, 22–23, 26–27, 28–29, 31; Wikipedia
Creative Commons: 23 (top), 23 (center), 23 (bottom).

Library of Congress Control Number: 2013920133

ISBN 978-1-909673-66-3

Printed and published in the United States of America

For further information including rights and permissions requests, please
contact our Customer Service Department at 877-337-8577.

# CONTENTS

# It's Going to Get Horrible!

The lives and habits of some animals can seem horrible to us humans.

There's the bot fly, for example. When it's a **larva**, or maggot, it lives inside another animal. Bot fly larvae have even been found living in animals' brains!

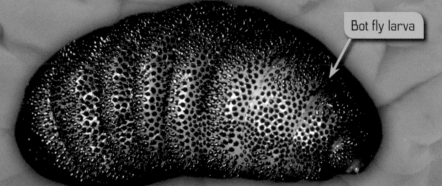

Bot fly larva

Then there's the Komodo dragon. This giant lizard catches its food using a deadly bite, killer drool, and lots of patience.

Komodo dragon

Dung beetle

And try to imagine living in poop and eating it. If you were a dung beetle, that's what you'd be doing right now.

DINNER IS SERVED!

So get ready to see some horrible animal habits in action. You're going to be horrified. You're going to be grossed out. But most of all, you will be truly amazed!

IT'S A FACT!

# Dung Beetles

Dung beetles are insects that feed on dung.
Cow dung, elephant dung—it's all food to
a dung beetle.

A heap of elephant dung

Fresh dung contains lots of
liquid. It's this smelly poop soup
that adult dung beetles eat.

Some types of dung beetles are known as rollers.
These beetles roll the dung they find into balls.
Roller dung beetles roll their dung balls away
from a dung heap. Then they bury them in the
ground to feed on later.

Number of types
of dung beetles:
**OVER 6,000**

A roller dung beetle rolling a dung ball

# Growing Up in Poop

When it's time to mate, a pair of roller dung beetles makes and buries dung balls. Then, after mating, the female lays an egg inside each ball.

Female dung beetle

Male dung beetle

A larva hatches from each egg. To help it grow, the larva eats the dung all around it.

Larva

Dung ball

The horrible habits of dung beetles are actually very helpful. The poop they bury in the ground is filled with **nutrients** that help plants grow. Also, these tiny animals help keep the world clean of poop.

DUNG BEETLES: HORRIBLE BUT HELPFUL HABITS!

# A Hippo's Horrible Habit

In the animal world, dung isn't just good to eat. It can have other uses, too.

Now, everyone likes their own space. Maybe you have a "keep out" sign on your bedroom door. An adult bull hippo is no different.

A bull hippo fighting

A bull hippo chooses a stretch of river to be his space, or **territory**. All the female hippos in that territory belong to him.

The bull must defend his territory from other males that will steal his females. One way to keep rivals away is to fight them. There is another way, too.

To mark his territory, a bull hippo uses a mixture of dung and pee!

He stands in water at the edge of his territory. Then he poops and pees at the same time. As he does, the bull hippo swings his tail from side to side. The tail chops up the poop and sprays it in every direction.

The bull hippo's stinky message tells his rivals all they need to know.

IT'S MY RIVER.
KEEP OUT!

# Komodo Dragons

A huge water buffalo staggers slowly from a forest. The animal is badly hurt. The buffalo's attacker follows just a few feet behind its victim.

Four days ago, the water buffalo was attacked by a Komodo dragon. The giant lizard tore at the buffalo's legs with its large, saw-like teeth. Deadly **toxins** in the dragon's spit are helping to kill the animal.

Komodo dragon

Now all the dragon needs to do is follow the water buffalo and wait for it to die.

Water buffalo

Length of a Komodo dragon: up to 10 feet long (3 m)

# A Dragon's Feast

Komodo dragons are the world's largest lizards. Using their savage bites, they can kill large **prey** such as deer and water buffaloes.

If a victim escapes, the dragon uses its sense of smell to track down the dying animal. A Komodo dragon smells through its long, forked tongue. It can smell its meal over 2 miles (3.2 km) away.

Once the dragon's victim finally dies, other dragons may join the feast. These giant lizards don't waste food. They eat hair, flesh, **entrails**, bones, hooves, and even horns!

Forked tongue

**DEADLY DRAGONS**

# Turkey Vultures

Komodo dragons do more than hunt live prey. They are also **scavengers** that eat animals that are already dead.

Turkey vulture

Scavengers do an important job. Without them, there would be lots of rotting **carcasses** around.

Turkey vultures are large scavenging birds. They feed on dead sheep and deer, and on road kill. Having a bald head is very helpful to these birds. Why?

# Please Pass the Napkins!

When feeding, a turkey vulture sticks its head deep into a carcass. It gets blood, flesh, and other body bits stuck to its head.

A bird can clean the feathers on its body with its beak. It can't clean its head, though. A bald head does not get as dirty and sticky as a head covered with feathers.

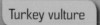

Turkey vulture

A rotting sea lion carcass

Standing on and in carcasses gets a turkey vulture's legs mucky, too. To kill off any germs from the carcass, a turkey vulture pees on its legs. On a hot day, this horrible habit also helps the bird cool off.

BALD, CLEAN, AND COOL!

# Bot Flies, Beyond Gross!

The habits of this next tiny animal are so gross you probably don't even want to read about them. Oh. You do?

Bot flies spend part of their lives inside the bodies of other animals. Sheep, horses, and even humans can all become homes for bot fly larvae.

An adult bot fly

A female horse bot fly lays her eggs on a horse's legs. A tiny larva hatches from each egg. Then it crawls into the horse's mouth. Here, the larva burrows into the horse's tongue or gums.

Bot fly eggs

Bot fly larva

# Stomach Invader

After about one month, the bot fly larva crawls from the horse's mouth into its stomach.

The larva attaches itself to the stomach with its hooked mouthparts. Here, the creature feeds on the horse's stomach for up to one year.

When it's time for the larva to become a fly, it lets go of the stomach. The larva travels through the horse's **intestines** and is pooped out by the horse. Inside a heap of horse dung, the insect becomes a **pupa**. Then, it changes into an adult fly.

IT'S GROSS, AND IT'S A FACT!

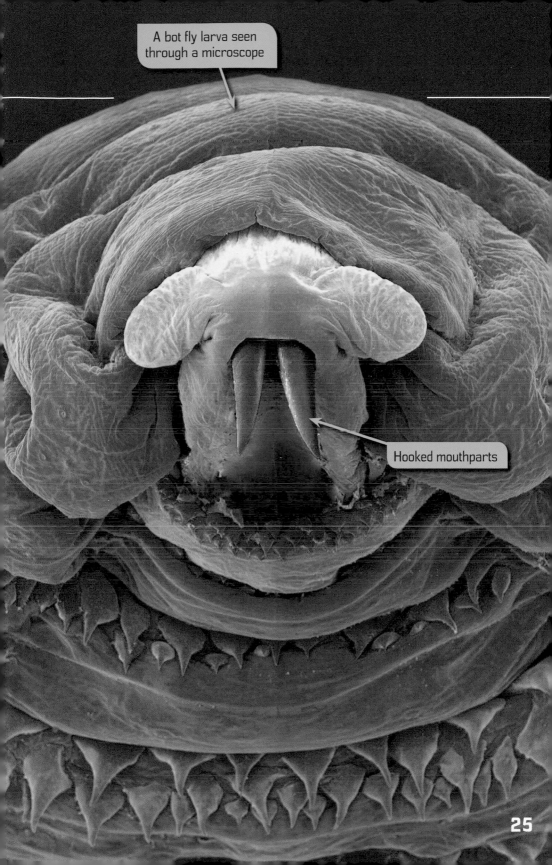

A bot fly larva seen through a microscope

Hooked mouthparts

# Dust Mites

Right now, trillions of tiny animals are hard at work, eating. It's the job of these little creatures to clean up the world around them.

The animals are eight-legged relatives of spiders.
Their bodies are nearly see-through. They are so tiny,
it's impossible for you to see them with your eyes alone.

These tiny creatures are dust mites. At this moment they
are living in the carpets, curtains, beds, sofas, and pillows
in your home. So how are they cleaning up the world?

A dust mite

# Dinner for Dust Mites

All around you in your home, tiny dust mites are eating your old skin!

Every minute, about 40,000 tiny bits of dead skin fall off your body. In your bed tonight you will be joined by millions of dust mites. Just think, as you sleep, the mites will be busy cleaning up tiny flakes of you!

# Glossary

**carcass** (KAR-kuhss)
A dead body. This word is usually used to describe the dead body of an animal.

**entrails** (EN-traylz)
The intestines, and sometimes other inside body parts, of a person or animal.

**intestines** (in-TES-tuhnz)
The tubes in a person's or animal's body where food is digested, or broken down, and poop is made.

**larva** (LAR-vuh)
A young insect that looks like a fat worm. Many insects have four life stages, which are egg, larva, pupa, and adult.

**nutrient** (NOO-tree-uhnt)
A substance that a living thing, such as a plant or animal, needs to grow, get energy, and stay healthy.

**prey** (PRAY)
An animal that is hunted by other animals for food.

**pupa** (PYOO-puh)
The stage in an insect's life when it changes
from a larva to an adult.

**scavenger** (SCAV-in-jer)
An animal that usually eats the carcasses
of dead animals. Some types of scavengers eat
poop or dead plants.

**territory** (TER-uh-tor-ee)
An area that belongs to an animal.
An animal might defend its territory from
rivals to protect the food in the area or to
protect its mates.

**toxin** (TOK-sin)
A poisonous substance that can harm or kill
a living thing.

# Index

# Read More

**Masoff, Joy.** *Oh, Yuck! The Encyclopedia of Everything Nasty.* New York: Workman Publishing Company, Inc. (2000).

**Owen, Ruth.** *Gross Body Invaders (Up Close and Gross: Microscopic Creatures).* New York: Bearport Publishing (2011).

# Learn More Online

To learn more about horrible animal habits, go to
**www.rubytuesdaybooks.com/horriblehabits**